Julie

Polly Stenham's plays include *That Face* (Royal Court and the Duke of York's), for which she was awarded the 2008 Critics' Circle Award for Most Promising Playwright, the *Evening Standard* Award for Most Promising Playwright 2007 and TMA Best New Play 2007; *Tusk Tusk* (Royal Court); *No Quarter* (Royal Court); and *Hotel* (National Theatre).

August Strindberg (1849–1912) was a Swedish dramatist, novelist, poet and essayist. His other plays include *The Father* (1887), *The Stronger* (1890), *Easter* (1900), *The Dance of Death* (1900), *A Dream Play* (1902) and *The Ghost Sonata* (1907).

T0313551

also by Polly Stenham from Faber

THAT FACE
TUSK TUSK
NO QUARTER
HOTEL

POLLY STENHAM

Julie

after

STRINDBERG

FABER & FABER

First published in 2018
by Faber and Faber Limited
The Bindery, 51 Hatton Garden
London EC1N 8HN

Reprinted with revisions 2018

A CIP record for this book
is available from the British Library

Typeset by Country Setting, Kingsdown, Kent CT14 8ES
Printed and bound by CPI Group (UK) Ltd, Croydon, CR0 4YY

ISBN 978-0-571-34959-3

Julie was first performed on the Lyttelton stage of the National Theatre, London, on 31 May 2018. The cast, in order of speaking, was as follows:

Julie Vanessa Kirby
Jean Eric Kofi Abrefa
Kristina Thalissa Teixeira

Partygoers Temitope Ajose-Cutting,
El Anthony, Thomasin Gülgeç,
Francesca Knight, Dak Mashava,
Michela Meazza, Beatriz Meireles,
Ashley Morgan-Davies, Rebecca Omogbehin,
Yuyu Rau, Petra Söör
Supernumeraries Subika Anwar-Khan, Steven Bush,
Holly Rose Hawgood, Tom Kelsey, Olivia Leat,
Tucker McDougall, Josefine Reich, Elliott Rogers,
Sophie Spreadbury, Miyuki Watanabe

Director Carrie Cracknell
Designer Tom Scutt
Lighting Designer Guy Hoare
Movement Director Ann Yee
Music Stuart Earl
Sound Designer Christopher Shutt
Fight Director Owain Gwynn
Illusions Chris Fisher
Video Designer Mogzi Bromley-Morgans
Company Voice Work Jeannette Nelson
Staff Director Jo Tyabji
Associate Movement Director Michela Meazza

Characters

Julie
thirty-three

Jean
thirty-one

Kristina
thirty

Partygoers

Author's Note on Casting

In this version Kristina is from Brazil and Jean is from
Ghana. This is by no means prescriptive, although
I imagine them to have emigrated to London in search
of work or sanctuary. Any references in the text to their
origins may be changed accordingly.

JULIE

For

4 The Grove

A birthday party rages throughout a large London townhouse. Julie whirls through the middle of chaos, greeting some guests, dancing with others. As the night progresses her actions start to become more manic, there's a harder edge to her pleasure seeking. People start to peel away, leaving the more darkly hedonistic guests and hangers-on. It's getting late. Julie doesn't want the party to end.

The kitchen. Kristina washes glasses. The party continues upstairs.
    Jean enters. He carries a tray of empty glasses.

Jean That woman is wild tonight.

    He sets the tray next to the sink.

Wild.

    Kristina unloads the tray.

Kristina You don't need to help.

Jean I might as well. If I'm here.

    He checks his phone, Kristina watches. He puts it back in his pocket.

Kristina Nothing?

    Jean shakes his head.

He's her father. He should be here. He should have been here hours ago.

Jean It's not his fault.

Kristina Even just for the toast. He could have left after that. She wouldn't have minded –

Jean Can't she have more fun without her father here anyway? She certainly seems to be.

Sounds of Julie cheering and turning up the music.

Kristina I don't think . . .

Jean What?

Kristina That's true.

Jean She was dancing with the bartender again. Dragging him around the room. As he was trying to leave.

Beat.

It's embarrassing.

Kristina Have you paid him?

He nods.

Jean Then she danced like a . . . I've never seen anything like it.

Kristina How many people are left?

Jean Ten. Maybe fifteen.

Kristina She's always been . . . Technicolor . . . But . . .

Jean But?

Kristina I think the breakup's hit her harder than she lets on.

Another whoop from upstairs.

Jean She doesn't exactly seem heartbroken.

Kristina She's ashamed.

Jean I don't believe that.

Kristina You wouldn't.

Jean What do you mean?

Kristina You know exactly what I mean.

Jean No, I don't.

Kristina You're a man.

Jean You're saying women feel more shame than men? That's a bold statement.

Kristina Yes.

Jean Why?

Kristina The world's been built that way.

Jean I saw what happened. When they broke up.

Pauses.

Jean Fine. If you don't want to know.

Kristina Tell me.

Jean He broke it off. Not nicely. Then she begged him to take her back.

Kristina Really?

He nods.

Poor girl.
   Where were they?

Jean The garden.

Kristina And you don't think she's ashamed?

Jean If she were ashamed she wouldn't have begged. Shame stops you doing things like that. That's the point of it.

Kristina runs her hand along the back of Jean's head.

Kristina It's a bit uneven.

He feels for her hand. Holds it.

Jean (*playful*) Is that so?

Kristina smiles.

Kristina That is so.

Jean So . . .

He pulls her closer. Close.

What did you save me?

Kristina holds a beat of tension between them, then slips away and opens the fridge. She takes out a plate of food from the party. It is covered in foil.

Thank you.

He peels the foil off.

It's cold.

Kristina You're getting comfortable, aren't you?

He's hurt.

Jean I didn't mean it like that –

Kristina I was joking.

She strokes his head affectionately.

I love you. *Amorzinho.*

Jean says nothing but smiles.
    He eats. Kristina opens a bottle of beer for him.
    Jean looks at it then puts his fingers to his lips. He takes out a bottle of red wine.

Kristina No. No. No –

Jean He won't notice. Even if he does he'll think it was one of them –

Kristina He'll notice.

Jean He won't. I'm driving. I can only have one drink. If I can only have one drink I want it to be a good one. Life's short don't you know?

Kristina Do you know how much that costs? He will.

He tastes the wine.

You're crazy.

Jean Beautiful. Wrong temperature though.

Kristina starts making a bowl of leftovers. She adds some drops to the bowl. He takes a sip of the wine and smiles. He comes over.

What's that?

Kristina offers him a spoonful.

Kristina Want some?

Jean What is it?

Kristina She's trying to give Diana an abortion.

He makes a face.

Jean With that?

Kristina It's some homeopathic. I don't know. Expensive though.

She holds the bottle up to the light.

For coloured water.

She looks at it more closely.

Those people are taking her for a ride. I wonder how much they sell it for . . .

She poses with the bottle.

Would you buy this from me? If I looked very, very serious?

Jean I'd buy air from you.

Kristina blows her breath at him, slowly.

Poor dog. She should just take her to the vet.

Kristina Not when she thinks 'western medicine' is the root of all evil. And if it's too evil for Julie it's too evil for Diana. She loves her animals like babies. That insane bird –

Jean She doesn't take medicine at all? Even if she's sick?

Kristina Not any more. Although she still likes a Xanax or two. I've seen them hidden in her red make-up bag. She thinks she's being discreet. But she forgets.

Jean What?

Kristina I clean up after her. I know everything.

Jean Everything?

Kristina Everything.

He comes closer.

Jean (*flirtatiously*) Do you need to do it now?

Closer.

Kristina Yes. She wants it done now.

Closer. They are about to kiss when there is another thump from upstairs. Something has been knocked over.

Jean Should I check?

Kristina shakes her head.

That sounded like furniture.

Kristina So?

Jean The way she was dancing I wouldn't be surprised if something got . . .

Kristina What?

Jean Broken.

Kristina I like to dance.

Jean I know.

Kristina steps closer.

Kristina Dance with me. When I'm finished.

Jean sniles.

Julie (*in the doorway, speaking offstage*) I'm coming
back. Stay there.

*Jean hides the bottle in the drawer; gets up respectfullly.
Julie enters. She wears a crown of flowers. She takes
it off to adjust it. She doesn't notice Jean.*

(*To Kristina.*) Have you done it? How is she?

Kristina Not yet.

Jean Has she done what?

Julie turns. She bats him with the crown of flowers.

Julie Stop it.

She stirs the mixture herself.

No peeping. Go away.

Jean Are you scared I'll learn your magic spells? What
are you trying to conjure?

Julie (*sharply*) Another lover. (*To Kristina.*) Actually, can
you give it to her in the morning?

Kristina Sure.

Julie Thank you thank you thank you. I just can't bear to
see it. You know. Happen. I don't think. Sorry.

She hugs Kristina and waltzes her around the room.

9

I'd be lost without you. Do you know that? Lost.

She kisses her cheek and rests her head on her shoulder. She squeezes her hand. Kristina squeezes back. The affection is genuine.

You're a star. Isn't she a star, Jean?

Jean She is.

Julie releases Kristina.
    She notices a bouquet of flowers on the counter.

Julie Let me guess. Couriered from office?

Kristina nods.

When?

Kristina A few hours ago.

Julie comes closer to the flowers.
    She picks them up and sniffs dramatically.

Julie Delicious. They smell like . . . (*Harder.*) Daddy's guilt.

She hands them to Kristina.

You have them.

Kristina But –

Julie They'll look nice in your room.

Music is turned up. Julie gestures to Jean.

Jean, come and dance.

Jean I should stay here.

Julie Lend me him, won't you, darling? It's the wild west up there.

Kristina It's not up to me.

Julie Come on then.

Jean I don't think I should.

Julie Why?

Slight pause.

If I'm going back up I want you to come with me. Perhaps that's vanity. In fact I'm sure it is. I want to look. I need to look . . .

Jean What?

Julie Wanted.

Jean looks uncomfortable. He's about to say something, then doesn't.

Don't look so serious.
　　Did you believe me? He believed me. I was teasing. Come on. Come and dance. It's my birthday, it's the solstice. Let's get pagan.

She takes his arm and leads him out of the room.

Don't worry. I won't steal him.

Julie and Jean exit to the party.
　　Kristina watches them go. She is still for a moment. She tidies Jean's plate and glass, then continues clearing up. She scoops the limes from the empty glasses. Empties glasses that have been used as ashtrays. Picks gum out of a real ashtray. Once she's cleared most of the kitchen she sits exhausted. She takes a mirror from her handbag. She opens it and stares at her reflection. She sighs. She puts the mirror back in her bag, She goes to the door and listens to the party. She spots a flower from Julie's flower crown on the floor. She picks it up. She puts it on the table. She looks at it pensively.

Jean enters alone.

Jean She's out of control.

Kristina She's fine. It's just late –

Jean People are laughing at her.

Kristina Laughing?

Jean They're not her friends. The people who are still here are not her friends.

Kristina What do you know?

Jean I see people coming and going, I have a rough idea.

She doesn't reply.

Are you angry with me?

Kristina shakes her head.
Wordlessly he pulls her to him. He wraps his arms around her. They kiss.
Julie enters. She watches them for a moment before speaking.

Julie What a charming man you are, abandoning your partner like that.

Jean puts his arm around Kristina.

Jean This is my partner.

Julie Why are you still wearing your suit? You look like you're going to court. Take the jacket off at least.

Jean Why?

Julie It's my birthday party. There's a theme. That suit is spoiling the salubrious atmosphere.

Beat.

I said take it off.

Beat.

Jean exits.

Where's he going?

Kristina To hang it in the car.

Julie pours them both a drink.

Julie (*suddenly serious*) How are you?

Kristina I'm fine.

Julie Are you really?

Kristina Yes.

Julie Good. Good. You seem it. You seem well.

Julie finishes her drink. Kristina doesn't touch hers.

Kristina Are you having fun?

Julie (*light, as if joking*) It's absolute hell.

Kristina keeps clearing up.

Please don't. Honestly. I'll do it before bed.

Kristina pauses. Julie takes her in.

Julie You look happy.

Kristina Do I?

Julie There's a sort of low-level eye twinkle. You're shinier somehow.

Beat.

So is he.

Beat.

I think he was miserable before he met you, you know. At least now he smiles. Once or twice a month.

She spies a textbook in the corner of the kitchen. She picks it up.

Brilliant! You're actually doing it! I'm so proud of you.

She flicks through it.

Looks hard. All that maths.

Is it math? Or maths?

She hands it back to her.

Is it hard?

Kristina It's okay so far.

Julie Do you like the teacher person?

Kristina He's nice. I think.

Julie Hot?

Kristina laughs.

Kristina No. Old.

Julie Old can be hot. Old can be golden.

Kristina I don't know. Not this guy.

Julie Do you have a picture?

Kristina That would be weird.

Julie Not these days. Everyone has pictures of everyone. Just put in a name and you can get a picture. Let's look him up.

Kristina No!

She pulls Julie's phone from her hand playfully.

You're an animal.

Julie Fine.
Spoilsport.

Kristina gives it back. Julie holds on to her hand when she does.

I admire you, you know.

Kristina Why?

Julie You get on with things. You're good at it.

She offers Kristina a cigarette. Kristina shakes her head.

Kristina I quit.

Julie You said that last time.

Kristina I've really quit.

Julie (*genuine*) Well done.

On an impulse she takes Kristina's face in her hands.

See. Good.

Julie lights hers.

Have you set a date?

Kristina No. Not yet.

Julie You should use our country place. There's a chapel there. I could even help you arrange it all. I'd love that. So would Father. In fact, he'd love it so much he might even turn up.

Kristina I think we want something small.

Julie I'm sorry I was so rude to Jean just then. I don't know what's wrong with me at the moment. It's as though when I open my mouth someone else has the keys to what I'm saying. Like I'm a sort of puppet of the worst version of myself. Does that make sense? It's as though my mouth opens and I –

Kristina (*gentle, kind*) It's okay.

They are still for a moment. Then Julie looks up.

Julie Do you even like me?

Before she can answer Jean re-enters; he has put a flower in his shirt buttonhole.

Très gentil, monsieur Jean. *Très gentil.*

Jean V*ous voulez plaisanter, madame.*

Julie *Et vous voulez parler français.* Where did you learn that?

Jean My mother's from Côte d'Ivoire. Where did you?

Kristina's phone rings. She answers, speaking Portuguese. She goes to a room off the kitchen to continue the conversation. It becomes clear she is speaking to a child.

Julie She sounds excited.

Jean Her son started school today.

Julie That's wonderful. In Salvador?

Jean nods.

Such a beautiful place.

Beat.

Have you been there?

Jean Not yet.

Beat.

Julie You look better without the jacket.

Jean You flatter me.

Julie Flatter you?

Jean (*dry*) You either exaggerate or have an agenda. Either way. Flattery.

Julie You can be rather formal, can't you?
Is it all those long drives with Daddy whispering in the

16

back seat? I bet you pick up a phrase or two in your line of work. A phrase or three.

He doesn't reply.

How long have you been working here?

Jean You know how long I've been working here.

Julie Do I?

Jean Yes.

Julie Not exactly.

Jean You had just left university.

Julie Which one?

Jean Five years ago.

She thinks.

Julie You're right. It was then.
We've known each other a long time.

Jean In a way.

Julie What do you mean 'in a way'?

Jean In that we don't really know each other at all.
Although I remember you. Then. I have a particular memory.

Julie Of what?

Beat.

Of what?

Jean I'll tell you another time.

Julie There might not be another time.

Kristina laughs loudly down the phone. Julie nods in her direction.

Julie She's good.

He doesn't reply.

Is she? Good?

He doesn't reply.

Sit down.

Jean (*sarcastic*) Am I allowed to?

Julie Don't be ridiculous.

He stares at her for a beat, then sits.

Wait.

We hear Kristina still on the phone as she takes the dog out.

Pass me something to drink first.

Jean What do you want?

Julie Whatever's left.

He rifles for a drink, finds a half-empty bottle of champagne. He pours her a glass.

Thank you.

She holds it.

Aren't you having one?

He doesn't reply.

I don't want to drink on my own.

Jean I'm driving.

Julie It's one drink.
Go on.
She won't mind.

Jean hesitates, then pours himself a glass.

Thank you. Let's toast.

Jean To what?

Julie To me.

He raises his eyebrows.

Do you think that's narcissistic?

He doesn't reply.

It is my birthday after all. The day of my birth. Someone should toast me. And given the circumstances, it might as well be me.

Jean doesn't move.

Don't make me beg.

He raises his glass.

Julie To Julie.

Julie Thank you.

They stay in position for a moment. There is the sound of someone running past the kitchen door. Jean springs up.

Jean They're not your friends, you know.

Julie What do you mean?

Jean You didn't notice how some of them were looking at you? What they were saying?

Julie What were they saying?

Jean hesitates.

Tell me.

Jean I don't want to hurt you.

Julie Then why bring it up? If you didn't want to hurt me then why bring it up?
I said tell me.

Jean You need to be more aware. In a room.

Julie What do you mean?

Jean You don't want people taking advantage.

Julie What if I don't care. If they take. Advantage.

They are close. Jean flicks an anxious look in the direction of Kristina's exit.

Jean This doesn't look good.

Julie What?

Jean Us. Drinking together. Alone.

Julie Don't be so Victorian. Relax. It's fine.

She opens her wallet and racks up two lines. She does hers. He doesn't do his. She stares at him challengingly. After a moment she does his too.

You look worried.

He doesn't reply.

Are you? Worried?

He doesn't reply.

Your face . . .

He checks his phone. Nothing.

Are you waiting to be summoned?

He doesn't reply.

You are, aren't you?

Jesus. Can't he just get a taxi for once?
Anyway, doesn't it get boring? The whole beck-and-call thing.

Jean This looks –

She inches closer, he moves away.

Julie What does it look like?

Jean Inappropriate.

Julie . Why? Have you made yourself believe something?

A Partygoer stumbles into the room, they move apart.
The Partygoer grabs a drink from the side and exits.

Jean It's not as simple for me.

Julie What?

Jean This

Julie That's a little dramatic, don't you think?

Jean Is it?

Julie Yes.

Beat.

Perhaps I think more highly of 'people' than you do.

Jean I imagine you do.

Julie I said perhaps.

Jean smiles.

Why are you smiling?

Jean Do you really want to know?

Julie I asked, didn't I?

Jean Because you're naive.

Julie I know.
Do you think I don't know that?
But I don't think that's the right word.
Really.
For what I am.

Jean What is?

Julie 'Strange'.
  I feel.
  Strange.

Jean You're strange then.

Julie Thank you.

  She takes him in.

So are you.
  So is everything.
  I mean, what is this, what's going on? What are we
doing?

  She touches her own skin.

What are we?

  She shivers.

Strange.

  Beat.

All of it.

  Beat.

And the more you think about it. The stranger it gets.

Jean What?

Julie Everything.

Jean What do you mean?

Julie I have this recurring dream. I dream that I'm inside
something warm and dark. I can't really move. But that's
alright. I feel. Good. In the warm dark. I can't tell where
I end or begin because whatever is pressing against me
also is me. I'm everything and nothing. Atomised. In the
dark. But then I hear a sound. It starts quietly. Just a little

scratching. But then it gets louder and louder and it sounds like metal on china like forks on plates like hundreds of people's cutlery scraping and banging on empty plates. Then the light comes and whatever was keeping me still isn't there any more. My arms flail slick with something except they're not arms they're wings and when I try to scream all I can hear is a rasping screech.

And just once, when I woke from this dream. There was a feather in my mouth.

It must have been from my pillow.

Have you ever dreamt anything like that?

Jean No. I usually dream I'm in a room.

Julie What kind of room?

Jean You know, a room. In a house.

Julie I know what a room is. What do you think the dream is *about* –

Jean I was trying to explain.

Julie Sorry. Go on.

Jean I dream that I'm in a room. Sometimes it's empty. Sometimes it's not. Sometimes there's a person there. Just behind me. Standing just behind me. I can feel them breathing. On my neck.

Julie Who?

Jean I don't know. I never know.

Beat.

Julie Why are we standing here talking about dreams? We're awake, let's be awake! Let's go on the roof. Let's watch the sun come up.

She has climbed on to the kitchen counter, and in the action a glass smashes. She is about to hop back down, close to the broken glass, when Jean stops her by picking her up and carrying her to the other side of the room. As he does so she bites his neck, lightly. He puts her down.

Jean What are you doing?

Julie I don't know what you mean.

Jean Don't play the child at thirty-two.

Julie I'm thirty actually.

Fine. Thirty-three.

Like Jesus.

Jean Stop. I mean it.

Julie (*mock horror*) I'm almost afraid.

They hear Kristina coming. They move apart. Kristina enters.

Jean How was he?

Kristina Okay.

She turns to them.

I think.

None of his friends are in his class. But he'll get used to that. Make new ones. Anyway.

Kristina makes to help clear up the glass.

Jean No, I've got it.

Kristina I've trained him well.

Is there anything else?

Julie shakes her head.

Are you sure?

Julie No. Thank you. You've been brilliant.

Beat.

I'm sorry it's gone on so late.

Kristina As long as you've had fun.

Beat.

Well, if you don't need anything. I'm going to bed.

Small pause. Jean doesn't move. Kristina kisses Jean goodnight.

(*To Julie.*) Well, don't stay up too late.
(*To Jean.*) Let me know when everyone's gone.

She exits.

Jean She's right. It's late.

Julie Or early.

Over this sequence Julie dims the lights. She plays a song on her phone. She pours another drink and dances a little to the music.

Jean Late.

Julie Technically, it's early.

Jean I should eject the final guests.

Julie Why would you do that?

Jean Because I don't want to leave you with those people still here.

Julie My 'friends'.

Jean Go to bed.

Julie You're not my nanny.

Jean Then don't act like you need one.

Jean Do you want him to see you like this when he comes back? I don't think that's a good idea –

Julie Who's to say he's coming back at all? He was meant to be here hours ago.

Beat.

Who's to say his merger hasn't turned into a little celebration in his pied-à-terre behind the office?

She watches his expression.

You think I don't know about that place?

He says nothing.

My point is, who's to say we haven't actually got all the time in the world?

Jean takes out his phone as she's talking. Nothing.

See?
So you can't use that excuse.
Not yet. Anyway.

Jean He's not a bad man.

Julie Excuse me?

Jean I said he's not a bad man.

Julie That depends, doesn't it? On your definition of bad.

Beat.

And I'm starting to suspect your definition is a little.
Loose.

Beat.

Sorry. I'm showing off now, aren't I? I'm being garrulous.

Beat.

Jean He's working. He works hard.

Julie I sort of prefer the alternative, to be honest. At least then he's having some fun. If he's not going to show up he might as well be tearing some girl apart on those Egyptian cotton sheets.

They're four hundred count. I saw the receipt.

There's the sound of a group of people leaving. Julie cocks her head to listen.

People are going now anyway. There's another party.

Jean Now?

Julie East. Well, the dregs of one.

They listen. The house sounds quiet.

See.

Jean I should check the house is secure.

Julie (*mocking*) That the house is secure?

Jean Yes.

Julie The house is fine.

Jean It's my job to make sure it's secure.

Julie Your job is to drive my father. Why are you even here tonight anyway? Oh sorry, I forgot. You're sticking the maid.

He stands. Angry.

Joking. I was joking.

Beat.

She's not technically the maid.

Jean I'm here because he asked me to make sure this didn't get out of control. I'm here because I'm working.

Julie You could have waited in the car. I would have let you know if anything happened. You didn't have to sit down here all night long –

Jean Yes. You're right. I should have done.

He makes to leave.

Julie I didn't mean that.

He stops. Turns.

I'm sorry.

He nods but continues leaving.
He stops.

Julie (*desperate.*) Have you ever felt like this?

Jean Like what?

Julie This . . .

She can't find the word.

Jean What?

Julie Alone.

Jean I don't understand.

Julie I didn't think so.

Jean Why are you asking me that?

Julie Because you seem happy.

Jean Do I?

Julie Yes.

Beat.

Well, sort of.

Jean What's that got to do with it?

Julie Tell me I'll feel better.
(*Desperate,*) Tell me I'll feel better.

Jean You'll feel better.

Julie You don't know that. No one can actually know that.

Jean These things pass.

Julie I don't know if they do.

Jean I've felt lonely from it before.

Julie What?

Jean People. Love.

Julie You?

Jean Why are you surprised?

Julie You don't exactly seem like someone who gives much away.

Jean You don't know me.

Julie I said 'seem'.

Julie Who was it?

Jean is silent.

Who was she?

He hesitates. She retracts.

Fine –

Jean You.

She steps back.

Julie How funny.

Jean That was what I didn't want to tell you before.

Julie When? When did you feel like that?

Jean I'd been driving your father for a few months. Then one day he invited me inside the house. He'd never done that before. Normally I'd wait outside but. This time he took me into the drawing room. From the window I could

see the garden. It seemed to stretch forever. Your land.
I thought how could anyone have so much land in a city.
How is that possible?

Julie The garden joins the Heath. It doesn't *all* belong to
us. That would be ridiculous –

Jean The sun was so bright that day. The garden. The
colours. It looked like Eden.
   Your father could see me staring. He told me I could
take a look around the garden. I thought he'd come with
me but then the phone rang and he waved me away. I
walked out of the garden doors and down the stone
steps. I walked down the path and I saw the summer
house. I didn't know what it was for, but I had never seen
such a beautiful building. A building just for. Pleasure.
The door was left open. I sneaked in and saw that the
walls were covered with photographs. I felt strange being
in there alone. As if I was hiding. As if the people in the
photographs were watching.

Julie Maybe you were.

Jean What?

Julie Hiding.

Jean I stepped outside again. I thought I'd come to the
end of the garden. I was about to turn back to the house
but then I saw more steps. They were almost hidden. I
stepped down them to see a whole second tier of garden
more wildly planted then the first. And in the middle of
this, almost secret garden. I saw you.
   The sunlight cut across your face.
   You were.

Julie What?

Jean Half smiling.
   I had never seen someone look so . . .
   Right.

Julie When was this?

Jean I told you. When I first started.

Julie I wonder what I was doing there.

Jean There were pieces of paper haloing your head.

Julie Ah. I was still writing.
You should have said hello. Introduced yourself.

Jean I didn't want to spoil it.

Julie Spoil it?
That's a strange way to put it.

Pause. She comes closer.

It's been hard for you, hasn't it? Coming here so young.

He seems about to say something but doesn't. Small pause. When he speaks he sounds almost amused.

Jean Courage is the first of human qualities because it is the quality that guarantees the others.

Julie Plato.

Jean Aristotle.

Julie Well-read too.

Jean Is that a surprise?

Julie No.

Jean It is, isn't it?

Julie No, it isn't.

Jean Yes, it is.

Julie Don't.

Jean I listen too. I learn a lot from listening.

Julie Do you sit there in the car listening to what we say?

Jean Wouldn't you?

Jean Once I heard you and your friend . . .

Julie Oh no –
What did you hear?

Jean That would be telling.

Julie Oh God.

Jean It wasn't that bad.

Julie Good.

Jean Although it was a little loose.

She's hurt, he tries to backtrack.

It made me think.

Julie What?

Jean Perhaps there's not such a big difference between people as one thinks.

Julie steps towards him seductively.

Julie (*under her breath*) It's all a construct.

He steps back.

Let's go up on the roof and watch the sun rise.

Jean No.

Julie Why?

He doesn't reply.

Why?

Jean You should go to bed.

Julie Is that an order, sir?

Jean Go to bed.

Julie Are you ordering me?

Jean Go.

*There is a sudden eruption of noise outside. A gang of
Partygoers have been swimming in the pool and are
returning. They are calling for Julie.*

Julie Hide.

Jean I'll get rid of them.

Julie No, I don't want anyone to know I'm still here.

Jean Why?

Julie Because then they'll want to stay.

Jean I'll tell them to go.

Julie No. They'll leave if they can't find me. Just hide.

Jean makes for the door.
 Julie grabs his hand and pulls him towards her.

Please.

*She pulls him into another room. They kiss. The sex
unfolds as the last of the Partygoers enter the kitchen.
They raid the drinks and finish the drugs. Eventually
one gets a text about another party. The door slams.
The stage is empty for a few moments.*
 *Kristina enters. She sees that the kitchen is empty
but Jean's phone is on the table. One of Julie's shoes lies
abandoned on the floor. Kristina follows a sound into
another room. She sees Julie and Jean. She re-enters
the kitchen. After a moment she takes Julie and Jean's
glasses and washes them. She puts them to dry by the
sink. She exits, taking her coat with her.*

It is starting to dawn outside. The room slowly fills with light over the rest of the scene.

Julie enters. She sits down at the table. She reaches for her cigarettes; the pack is empty. She sees a half-finished one in the ashtray. She picks it out and lights it. Inhaling gratefully. Jean enters. She stubs it out.
Pause.

Julie What are we going to do?

Jean I don't know.

Julie Maybe we should run away.

Julie If this was a story we'd run away.

She is searching the room for more cigarettes. No luck.

Jean Where?

Julie Far.

Jean Cape Verde. Have you ever been there?

Julie No.

Julie Is it beautiful?

Jean Very.
Oranges on the trees.

Julie (*slightly mocking reference to earlier*) Eden?

Jean Close enough.

Julie What will we do there?

Jean Buy some land. Build something. A restaurant maybe.

Julie A restaurant?

Jean Why not? New faces all the time, never a minute looking for something to do. It wouldn't be boring. There's always something to do when you run a restaurant –

Julie Do you say this from experience?

Jean I've worked in a lot of places.

Julie What would I do? At this restaurant?

Jean You'd be the face of the place. You'd lure people in with your beauty. You'd suggest drinks and choose the music. You'd never get a single song wrong. You'd be the soul, the beating heart. Every morning we'd walk straight from the kitchen on to the beach, and then to the boats to choose fresh fish. You'd choose the most beautiful. The biggest. The heaviest. Pearly-scaled and dripping in my arms. Sand. Flashes of sun. You. Barefoot. Mine.

Julie You've thought about this, haven't you?

Jean We could get a plane in a few hours. We could be there by tonight.

Julie Do you love me?

Jean I want to.

Julie What does that mean? I thought you were 'sick' from the heartbreak of not having me? What the hell does that mean, you 'want to'?

Jean It means I can't love you in this house. Not properly.

Julie Why not?

He gestures around him.

Explain.

Jean Your father.

Julie What about him?

Jean It wouldn't work.

Julie What do you think he is? Some sort of . . .

Jean What?

Julie Tory?

Jean raises his eyebrows.

He's socially liberal.

Jean It just wouldn't work.

Julie Why?

Jean We could all pretend it would. But it wouldn't. Not really. Not properly.

Julie Then I have a better opinion of people than you do.

Jean Are you surprised?

She doesn't respond.

Look. Today I'm this. But by next year we could have a successful restaurant, then ten years after that we could be living off my investments.

Julie God. You're serious.

Jean Do you think I'm happy to settle just for this? This job is only a step. I'm saving money to buy land. Once I buy land I'll build, once I've built I'll employ people, once I employ people –

Julie You'll be like me.

Jean I'll never be like you.

Julie Why?

Jean Because I'll have earned it myself.

Julie If that wasn't so utterly true I'd be offended.

Jean Why did you think I was working here?

Julie Honestly, I hadn't given it much thought. I was too busy gagging on my silver spoon.

Jean Tell me what you thought.

Julie I don't know, I thought maybe you were sending money home to family or something.

His eyes widen.

What?

Jean Flies on the face. Dust. Is that what you imagine?

Julie That's not what I said.

Julie Stop looking at me like that.

Jean Like what?

Julie I don't know. Like that.

Jean We could do something real together, you know. Make something. Build something.

Julie How much have you thought about this?

Beat.

Could you love me?

Jean Yes.

They move towards each other. A moment's pause.

What do you think?

Julie Of what?

Jean Of my suggestion? Of leaving tonight.

Julie It was my suggestion actually.

Jean What do you think?

Julie I like it. I like it very much.

Beat.

We could go before he gets back. Before she wakes up.

He nods, she smiles, a flash of excitement between them. It's all possible.

How much money would we need? To start this place?

Jean Not that much. Compared to here. It's cheap there, land's a steal.

Julie Have you got any?

Jean Land?

Julie Money.

Jean I have other capital.

Julie What exactly?

Jean My skills, my experience –

Julie You can't buy a plane ticket with 'experience'.

Jean Which is why I seek a partner who can advance the funds.

She realises. Small pause.

Julie Where will you find one at such short notice?

Jean You must have –

Julie What? Have what? Ready cash? Connections?

He says nothing.

Why do you think I've moved back home? Do you think I'm back sleeping in my childhood bedroom because I'm such a success? Do you think this is a choice? Do you think if I had any money of my own I'd still be here?

Jean You can't have nothing at all.

Julie Everything I've inherited from her is in a trust.

Jean Everything?

Julie I can't be trusted with money. Don't you get it?

Jean Well then . . .

Julie Then?

Jean Things stay as they are.

Julie But we can't. This can't continue. If we stay here. It wouldn't be . . .

Jean What?

Julie Realistic.

Jean Because . . .?

Julie Because you have a girlfriend. Sorry, a *fiancée*.

Jean That's not what you meant.

Julie It is.

Jean You meant something else.

Julie No I didn't.

Jean You did. What did you really want to say?

Julie Nothing.

Jean That's not true.

Julie IT FUCKING IS.

Jean Be quiet.

Julie Are you scared we'll wake her?

Jean Please calm down.

Julie Okay. Yes. Okay.

Jean We need to be be rational. Practical. Make a plan.

Julie Rational? You want a rational experience, do you?

Nothing about any of this is rational, you're through the looking-glass now, and so am I –

Jean Sit down.

Julie Don't talk to me like that.

Jean Here, have a drink.

He pulls out the hidden wine.

Julie Where did you get that wine from?

He doesn't respond.

Is that my father's Château Latour?

He doesn't respond.

Even I don't touch that.

Jean Which just proves you have no taste.

Beat.

Julie (*light*) Thief.

Jean (*light*) If I'm a thief so are you.

Julie (*light*) Excuse me?

Jean What we just did to her is theft.

Julie doesn't respond.

You don't agree?

Julie Do you think I don't know that? She's my friend.

He raises his eyebrows.

Jean She's not your friend.

Julie Well, no one is my friend according to you.

Jean I don't think you read people very well. Or maybe it's that you choose not to. I can't work it out.

Julie People are people –

Jean And staff are staff.

Julie gestures around her.

Julie (*desperate*) This. This is not my fault.

He suddenly notices their two glasses have moved and are now washed up on the side of the sink.

Jean Did you move those?

Julie What?

Jean Those, our glasses, did you move them?

Julie I don't know. Maybe.

Jean Did you or didn't you?

Julie I was looking for cigarettes. I moved some things. I don't know.
No. I'm sure it was me. I'm always forgetting where I put things. I do it all the time.

Jean Stop talking. Please.

She does.

Are you sure it was you?

Julie Yes.

Beat.

Jean You know I wouldn't ever take something someone had only a little of. I wouldn't take something anyone would even notice being gone.

Julie You don't have to excuse it.

Jean Why?

Julie Because I get it –

Jean No, you don't –

Julie I get doing something you shouldn't just to feel a little better, a little more yourself.

Jean Why are you so unhappy?

Julie Goodness. Could that sentence drip with more contempt? You didn't even try and hide it.

Jean I'm curious.

Julie No, you're not. You're just looking for more reasons to find me pathetic and ridiculous and therefore absolve yourself of any responsibility –

Jean Responsibility for what?

Julie Of fucking me for my money. Shake me and I rattle. Is that what you think? Go on. Try. Shake me.

Jean Stop –

Julie Shake me –

Jean Acting like that.

Julie Like what?

Jean Like there's something wrong with you.

Julie I don't understand what you –

Jean If there's something wrong with you it gives your selfish actions some meaning and there's nothing worse than no meaning, is there? That's when the real fear starts. Because you're shapeless, aren't you? Sort of pointless. And it's terrifying.

Julie (*heated*) Is that your opinion?

Jean Yes.

Julie Is that your armchair analysis?

Jean Yes.

She's close to him now.

Julie Did it ever occur to you?
   That maybe I slept with you –

   Even closer.

42

(*Practically spits the words.*) Because I wanted to.

Beat.

I think you're afraid of me. Of this. You're afraid. You're afraid and it's PATHETIC. That's why you've gone for something so ordinaty, somethiong so SAFE.

Jean Actually I feel sorry for you.
I felt sorry for you then, too.

Julie When?

Jean Lying at the bottom of the garden. You thought you looked like you were in some sort of painting, didn't you? One of the oils in your father's study. Pre-Raphaelite. When actually you looked like any other lazy overgrown woman child. Asleep with her mouth open and a cigarette burning. Asleep on a Monday afternoon.

Julie You're lying.

He doesn't reply.

Stand up when I speak to you.
Get up.
GET UP.

Jean (*urgent, glancing at the door*) Lower your voice.

Julie I'm your employer. Stand up when I speak to you.

Jean Your father's my employer. Actually. Either way though, I could tell on you.

Julie For what?

Jean gestures at the drugs.

Jean It could make the papers. With a name like yours.
See. We can both pull rank.

Beat.

Darling.

43

Julie You wouldn't dare.

Jean Wouldn't I?

I've seen how you've looked at me. Over the years.
You look at me like I'm simple. Like I'm an animal. Like
you know what I want. So you play with it. Me.

It's never occurred to you, has it, that I can play with
you too?

And you act like I'm the crude one. I've never met
anyone who acted like you did tonight. I've seen animals
with more dignity . . .

He tails off.

Julie (*crushed*) Go on.
Finish.
(*Angry.*) I said. Go. ON.

He doesn't respond.

You're proud of it. What just happened. You wanted it too.

Jean Maybe.

Beat.

Although the conquest was a little too easy to give me
genuine pleasure.

Julie You can't see beyond the idea of conquest, can you?
You only see it, me, as a thing to have. You 'had' me.
That's what you think, isn't it? Which is ironic. Because if
anyone conquered anyone, if anyone had anyone. I had
you.

Small pause.

Jean What are we going to do?

Julie We're going to leave here. Together.

Jean To talk like this to each other forever?

Julie No. To enjoy ourselves. As long as we can. And then die.

Jean Die? No. Let's build our restaurant.

Julie In Cape Verde. Oranges on the trees.

Jean We could be there so soon.

She smiles at him. He smiles back.

Julie We could wake up there.
In one of those beds with the netting around it. Ocean breeze. No things. No things around us. No stuff. No things.
Just our bodies.
Clean sheets.
Warm.
Skin.

He closes his eyes as if imagining it.

Jean Do we have enough. For a flight? Just the flight? We could figure the rest out when we're there, we'd work it out somehow –

Julie Money money money –

Jean Why is it so dirty to you? Money? You can do something with what you have, don't you get that? Stop being ashamed. Own it. Own this. Use what you have to build something. To make something. To be strong.

Julie Money money money, then we die.

Jean (*genuine*) I don't want to die.

Julie Really?

Jean It scares me.

Julie I think it's like before being born. A sort of wonderful. Nothing.

Jean I think it could be worse.

Julie Hell?

He doesn't reply.

Oh my God, you believe in God.

He doesn't reply.

You do, don't you? Wow.

She laughs.

Jean Why are you laughing?

Julie I'm sorry, it's just a bit like someone believing in Santa, it's sweet actually.

She edges closer to him, pushes his hand between her legs.

What would your God make of tonight? Would he be thrilled?

He pulls away.

Jean I'm tired of this. I'm going to the car.

Julie You're tired, are you? You're done?

Jean This is stupid. We're being stupid –

Julie You think I can be brushed off like that? You owe me more than that –

Jean Do you know why your father really stayed away? It's because he hates seeing you like this. Out of control. Slurring. Popping pills. It reminds him of her. Before she did it. It's too painful. And you know that. Deep down you know that –

Julie You're right. It doesn't look good.

Jean What do you mean?

Julie People might not believe it was my choice.

He steps back.

Jean You shouldn't get high.

Julie Why?

Jean It makes you say things you don't mean.

Julie So?

Jean It makes you talk too much.

Julie I shouldn't talk? Is that what you'd like? You'd like me nice and mute? Is that how you'd like me? Nice and QUIET –

Jean Shhh . . .

She stares at him silently.

(*Dawning on him.*) You actually would. Wouldn't you?

Julie I didn't *say* anything. I just repeated what you said to me.

He steps back again, eyes wide.

Fine. I regret it. I regret the *insinuation*.

He doesn't respond.

I'm completely desperate. Don't you see –

Jean What do you want me to do? What is it you want from me? I don't understand. I don't understand you. Do you want me to cry? Kiss you? Take you away? And then what? This is getting painful. Look. I can see that you're miserable. I can see that in some way you've always been miserable. But I don't understand you. I don't have the luxury, we don't have the luxury of being sad like you. Love to me is a game I can play when I have a few hours off, I don't have all day and night like you do. It's not a blood sport to me. That's a luxury. To torment yourself like this is a luxury. To have the fucking time.

Julie stares at him.

Why are you looking at me like that?

Julie I want to do it. I want to be with you. Let's go.

Jean I'm here.

Julie Are you?

Jean I'm here. Let's go.

Julie I need a drink first.

Jean Do you really want to go?

Julie Yes. I do.

Jean Then we should go now, right now –

Julie I need to tell you something first –

Jean (*starting to get anxious about the time*) Kristina will get up soon –

Julie Please listen to me. I need you to know me properly, I need you to know me properly before we go –

Jean Any minute –

Julie LISTEN TO ME.
  She was a complicated woman. My mother.

She waits for him to say something. He doesn't.

You know I was the one to find her?

He says nothing.

Money isn't everything. And love is a joke.

Jean But you got engaged.

Julie Exactly. Ha ha.

Jean What happened?

Julie I got bored of him.

Jean That's not what happened, is it?

Julie What do you mean? What did he say?

He doesn't reply.

I broke it off. Has he said it was him? The liar.

Jean I saw you tell him you were tired. That you just wanted to rest. To stop looking.

Julie Cruel.

Jean It's what I saw.

Julie I hate you.

Jean Do you?

Julie I think I'd like to kill you. Like an animal.

Jean I'm sorry.

Julie No, you're not. You wanted me to be ashamed of loving. I will never be ashamed of loving. Of wanting. OF NEEDING. Fuck you.

She is close to him. Closer. Nearly kiss.
He notices Kristina's coat is gone.

Jean Where's her coat?

Julie Who's coat?

Jean Kristina's. She hung it up, before she went upstairs.

Julie Did she?

Jean Yes.

Julie Are you sure?

Jean Yes.

He exits.
Julie digs around in drawers looking for cigarettes.
She suddenly remembers where she hid some; she finds

the hidden, nearly empty packet. She lights one and inhales gratefully.

She digs into her make-up bag and pulls out a pill. She takes it quickly.

Jean re-enters.

Jean She's gone.

Julie What do you mean, gone?

Jean She's not in her room and her coat is gone.

Julie Maybe she's taken the dog out again.

He opens the door to the side room. The dog wakes up and starts barking manically. Jean then goes to the sink and picks up the glasses. He sees they've been washed.

Jean They're clean.

Julie So?

Jean Did *you* wash them up?

It dawns on her.

Julie You don't know that she saw –

Jean Why else would she leave –

Julie You don't know for sure –

Jean I do –

Julie How –

Jean BECAUSE SHE'S NOT FUCKING STUPID.

Julie Why do you care? If we're going to leave together, why do you care if she knows?

He doesn't answer.

What are we going to do?

Jean You could leave first.

Julie Me?

Jean Today. Travel. Go anywhere. Just for a while. Enough time for –

Julie For what? You to patch things up with your fiancée?

Jean Enough time for me to follow you, without it looking –

Julie No. I can't go alone. No. I won't do that.

Jean She could tell him. She'll be so angry, she could tell him –

Julie I'll go if you come with me.

Jean I'll follow you. I promise.

Julie Really?

Jean Really.

Julie I'm so tired. I'm so so tired. Just tell me what to do. I can't think any more.

Jean Go upstairs. Get dressed. Get what you need for the journey, then come downstairs.

Julie Come with me upstairs.

The room is starting to get light.

Jean Go quickly. I'll clear up down here. .
Go. Now.

He takes her hand and leads her offstage a little roughly .
She exits.
Jean is on his own. He starts tidying, getting rid of all evidence, then stops suddenly. And sits. Wordless. The room is now full of light. Julie enters carrying a birdcage covered with a towel.

Julie I can't leave him behind

Jean Put it down

Julie He won't look after him –

Jean That's insane, put it down –

Julie It's the only thing I'm taking.

Jean You can't bring that –

Julie I'm not leaving him here on his own –

Jean Put it down –

Julie HE WON'T LOOK AFTER HIM HE CAN'T LOOK AFTER HIM –

Jean So what?

Julie I can't leave him here, I can't, I won't –

Jean Put it down –

Julie I'd rather kill him –

Jean Fine go on –

Julie   I'd rather kill him

Jean Go on then.
Go on. FUCKING DO IT

Julie takes the bird out of the cage. She goes to the blender. She opens the lid. She puts the bird in the blender.
    After a few moments she goes to open it.

Jean Don't –

Julie Do you think I'm afraid? Do you think I'm afraid of that? Afraid of looking at it? Do you worry it might scare me?

She takes what she can of the bird out of the blender. Blood.

Thing is. When you've seen the worst thing. When you've had the worst thing. Happen. Nothing really frightens you again. Because what's really frightening. Is already inside you. It. IS. You.

She smears the blood on her face. He steps back. She looks towards the window. The brightening light.

It's so light.
Come with me.
Come with me.
Please. I can't be on my own today. A crammed plane. People staring at me. The queues, the headache, children screaming. No. I can't. I can't.
I can't stop remembering. Today. I can't stop. Remembering. Being a child. I keep having flashes of summer. Of afternoons in the garden. Of making strange things with sticks. Talking to animals. Bruises. The good kind of bruises. Not. These. Finding chocolate in my pocket melted in the wrapper so I could push and twist into new shapes and give to her. What's happened to me since then? What's happened to me? So much has happened but also nothing at all. Even if I run. Memories come and with them the guilt guilt guilt and what I've become.

He comes closer. They are nose to nose. She crumples into him. The moment is tender.

Julie You're not pretending?

Jean No. Let's do it, let's go. Now. Before she comes back.

Kristina enters. She holds a takeaway coffee.
Pause.

Kristina You've made a mess, haven't you?

Julie Listen to me, Kristina, listen to me and I'll tell you everything.

Kristina I don't want you to tell me everything.

Julie I can't stay here and Jean can't stay here. So we have to go.

Kristina I see.

Julie But I've had an idea.

Kristina And what's that?

Julie Why don't the three of us go together?

Kristina doesn't respond, Julie pushes on.

To Cape Verde. To open a restaurant together. Wouldn't it be good? We could run it together. I think together we could. It could be such a success, couldn't it? Our restaurant . . .

She tails off.

Kristina Do you believe that?

Julie Do I believe it?

Kristina Yes.

Julie No.

Kristina turns to Jean.

Kristina Are you insane?

Julie I don't know. I don't know

Kristina (*to Jean*) I wanted so badly for you to surprise me.

Jean I –

Kristina And I went to church with you. To please you.

Julie It was me. It wasn't him.

Jean That's not true.

Julie I started it. I'm sorry.

Kristina I hold your hair up when you're sick. I pick you up after your abortion. I wash your bloodstained underwear. I get up most days and I serve you. But I tell myself, it's not her fault. She's a nice girl. It could be the other way round. She treats me well. She treats me like a person. She didn't write history. She's just snared in the story like me. Sometimes she even makes it possible for us to both pretend that we're not hostage to our situation. Sometimes when we're talking in the kitchen we can both pretend that it's all pretend. And that makes the job, sort of bearable, that we both have moments of pretending. That it all isn't so fucked. That it all isn't so fucking unfair. You see all I had here, was a tiny bit of dignity. But even that you've snatched, and it wasn't even precious to you. I don't think you even knew I had it. That I need it. I don't think you know what it's like to need something. Just what it's like to want. And want. And want. Because, what you've done, what you've just done, is worse than sex with someone you shouldn't. That's child's play really. It's ordinary. It's the oldest trick in the book. What you've actually done is you've turned the light on. When we'd both agreed to sometimes have it off. In what you've done, you've reiterated everything. The taking, the taken. In your action is the whole world. You are wrong. You are what's wrong.

Julie I –

Kristina If I were you I'd go upstairs. Clean yourself up. You look awful.

> *Kristina exits.*
> *Pause.*

Julie She's right. I do.

> *She turns to Jean.*

Clean sheets, empty room. Let's go.

He doesn't respond,

Julie Are you angry with me?

Jean I've got to go

He exits.

The sunlight has reached the floor. Julie is alone on stage. She is still for a moment, then goes to the fridge, takes out a bottle of water and drinks from it. She sits down. She takes a pill. Sits for a moment, then takes three more pills. She fumbles for a cigarette. She lights it. After a minute she pulls the pills out from her make-up again. She takes another pill and grinds it up and snorts it. She stands. Closes her eyes. She feels her own heartbeat slow. We enter her experience. The light brightens. Everything slows.

Time passes.

Julie is slumped on the floor. Kristina enters holding several bags. She is about to leave. She doesn't see Julie at first. When she does she kneels and shakes her. She can't wake her. She tries to pull her upright but Julie slumps in her arms. She feels for her pulse. She stands and backs away slowly. She reaches for Julie's phone. She dials. As she waits for an answer she fumbles for one of Julie's cigarettes. The lighter flares. Darkness.

The End.